BABOON METAPHYSICS

and MORE Implausibly Titled Books

I think, therefore, I a

Aurum

First published in Great Britain 2009
by Aurum Press Ltd
7 Greenland Street
London NW1 0ND
www.aurumpress.co.uk

A catalogue record for this book is available from the
British Library.

ISBN 978 1 84513 498 3

10 9 8 7 6 5 4 3 2
2013 2012 2011 2010 2009

Interior design by David Fletcher Welch
Title page illustration by Glyn Goodwin,
www.glyngoodwin.co.uk
Printed in China

THERMAL MOVEMENTS IN THE UPPER FLOOR OF A MULTI-STOREY CAR PARK

A. Williams and S. W. Clements

Cement & Concrete Association, 1980

Detailed investigation into the behaviour of cracks.

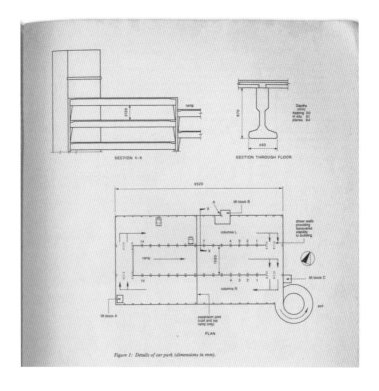

Figure 1: Details of car park (dimensions in mm).

TECHNICAL REPORT

539

Thermal movements in the upper floor of a multi-storey car park

A. Williams BA, CEng, MIMechE **and**
S. W. Clements HNC

October 1980

ILLUSTRATED ENCYCLOPEDIA OF METAL LUNCHBOXES

Allen Woodall & Sean Brickell

Schiffer Publishing Ltd, 1992

Showcasing the finest private collection in full colour.

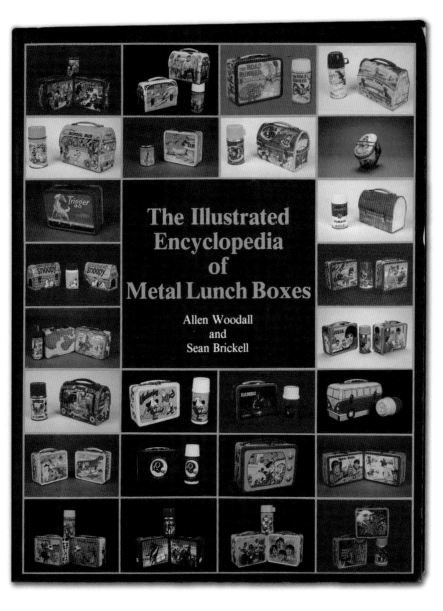

The Illustrated Encyclopedia of Metal Lunch Boxes

Allen Woodall
and
Sean Brickell

COOKING WITH GOD

Robert L. Robb & Lori David

Ermine Publishers, 1976

Cookery book.

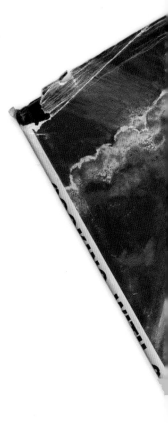

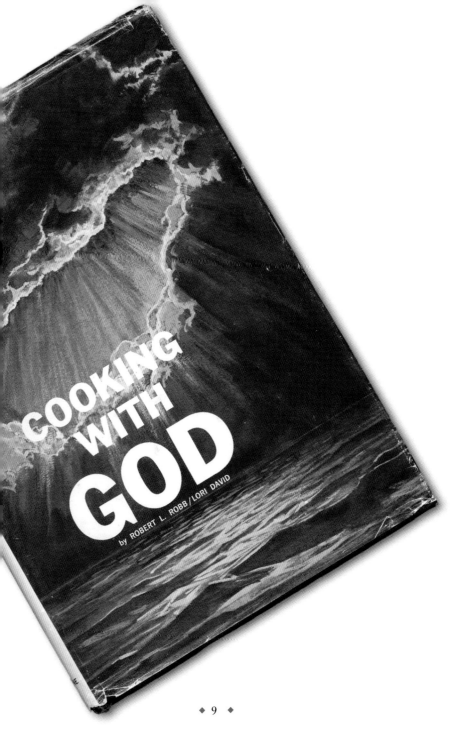

COOKING
WITH
GOD

by ROBERT L. ROBB / LORI DAVID

EAT YOUR HOUSE:
Art Eco Guide to Self-Sufficiency

Fredric Hobbs

Virginia City Restoration Corporation, 1980

Domestic self-sufficiency as an art form.

'The pollution-resistant greenhouse has become a symbol of freedom.'

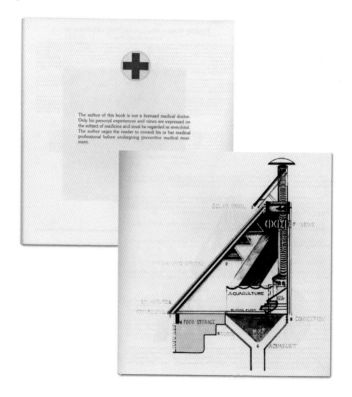

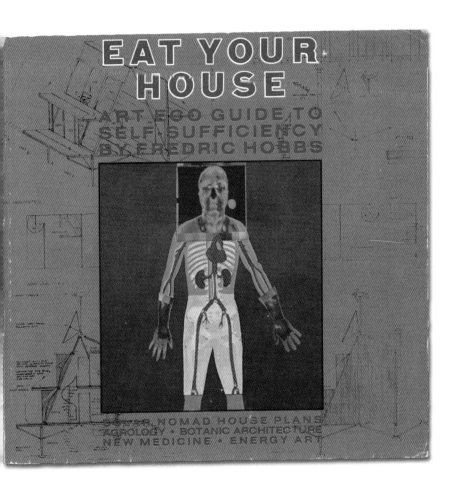

EAT YOUR HOUSE

ART ECO GUIDE TO SELF-SUFFICIENCY
BY FREDRIC HOBBS

NOMAD HOUSE PLANS
AGROLOGY • BOTANIC ARCHITECTURE
NEW MEDICINE • ENERGY ART

MARGARINE: An Economic, Social and Scientific History, 1869-1969

J. H. Van Stuyvenberg (editor)

Liverpool University Press, 1969

A crowded century for the non-fattening butter alternative.

EDITED BY J.H. van STUYVENBERG
Professor of Economic History, University of Amsterdam

Margarine

*An economic, social, and
scientific history, 1869–1969*

J. van ALPHEN J. BOLDINGH R. FERON
A. C. FRAZER W. G. HOFFMANN K. E. HUNT
J. H. van STUYVENBERG and R. D. TOUSLEY

Foreword by A. H. BOERMA, *Director-General, Food and Agricultural
Organization of the United Nations*

LIVERPOOL UNIVERSITY PRESS

ANCIENT STARCH RESEARCH

Robin Torrence & Huw. J. Barton (editors)

Left Coast Press Inc, 2006

Starch in archeology: how plant residue reveals the
hidden mysteries of food processing in the Stone Age.

ANCIENT STARCH RESEARCH

EDITED BY
ROBIN TORRENCE
& HUW BARTON

ORAL SADISM AND THE VEGETARIAN PERSONALITY:
Readings from the Journal of Polymorphous Perversity

Glenn C. Ellenbogen Ph.D.

Ballantine Books, 1988

Satirical look at the obscure language used by psychologists.

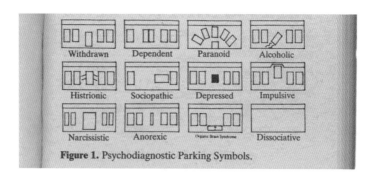

Figure 1. Psychodiagnostic Parking Symbols.

BB Ballantine/Humor/34700/$3.95

ORAL SADISM AND THE VEGETARIAN PERSONALITY

Readings from the
Journal of Polymorphous Perversity®

Edited by GLENN C. ELLENBOGEN, Ph.D.

"YOU'LL LOVE THIS ONE!"
The Psychotherapy Newsletter

D. DI MASCIO'S DELICIOUS ICE CREAM: D. Di Mascio of Coventry - an Ice Cream Company of Repute, with an Interesting and Varied Fleet of Ice Cream Vans

Roger de Boer (author), Alan Wilkinson (compiler) & Harvey Francis Pitcher (editor)

Past Masters, 2006

Obscure corner of the Transport book market.

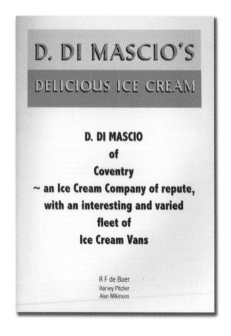

D. DI MASCIO'S

DELICIOUS ICE CREAM

Roger de Boer
Harvey Pitcher
Alan Wilkinson

GUT REACTIONS: Understanding Symptoms of the Digestive Tract

W. Grant Thompson

Da Capo Press Inc, 1989

Handbook for avid students of their own internal functions.

A COLOUR ATLAS OF POSTERIOR CHAMBER IMPLANTS

Arthur S. M. Lim

W B Saunders Company, 1985

Graphic step-by-step techniques of intraocular implant surgery.

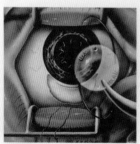

Fig. 8.9
Examination of implant.

Fig. 8.10
Insertion of inferior loop into anterior chamber.

Fig. 8.11
Placement of inferior loop behind iris (anterior to anterior capsule).

Fig. 8.12
Flexing superior loop with forceps.

A COLOUR ATLAS OF
POSTERIOR CHAMBER IMPLANTS

Arthur S. M. Lim

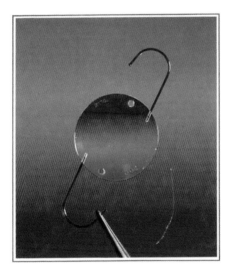

Contributors:
J. Alpar, C.D. Binkhorst, R.C. Drews, W. S. Harris,
D. J. McIntyre, M. J. Roper-Hall, C. W. Simcoe.

SAUNDERS

NASAL MAINTENANCE: Nursing Your Nose Through Troubled Times

William Alan Stuart

McGraw-Hill, 1983

Guide to good nasal health.

Figure 11. The allergic salute: stop-action sequence

Figure 19. Creating a steam tent

>>$6.95

nasal

MAINTENANCE

Nursing Your
Nose
Through
Troubled
Times

WILLIAM ALAN STUART, MD

THE PROSTATE: A Guide for Men and the Women who Love Them

Prof. Patrick C. Walsh MD
& Ms. Janet Farrar Worthington

The Johns Hopkins University Press, 1995

Ideal gift for husbands or, alternatively, for fascinated wives.

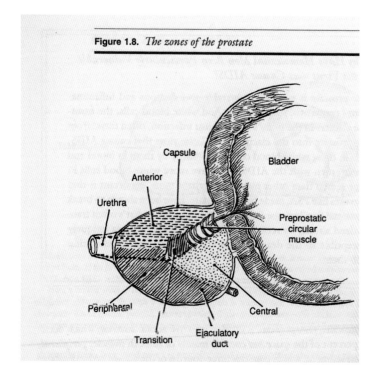

Figure 1.8. *The zones of the prostate*

THE FACTS YOU NEED

Cancer • Enlargement • Infection

THE

Prostate

A GUIDE FOR MEN
AND THE WOMEN
WHO LOVE THEM

Patrick C. Walsh, M.D.
Urologist-in-Chief, The Johns Hopkins Hospital

Janet Farrar Worthington
Science Writer

A JOHNS HOPKINS HEALTH BOOK

WHY REPLACE A MISSING BACK TOOTH? (Educate Your Patients)

Joel M. Berns

Quintessence Publishing Co Inc., 1994

Attempts to answer the question that rarely troubles the majority of dental patients.

Why Replace a Missing Back Tooth?

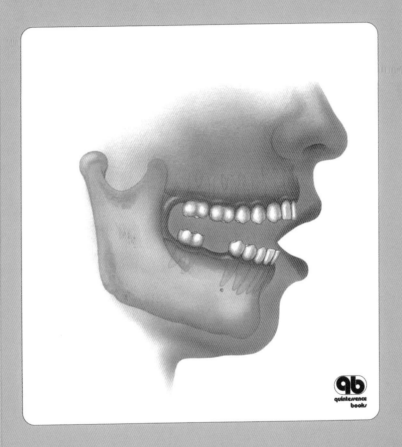

quintessence books

Joel M. Berns, DMD

SHORT-TERM VISUAL
INFORMATION FORGETTING

A. H. C. van der Heijden

Routledge & Kegan Paul Ltd, 1981

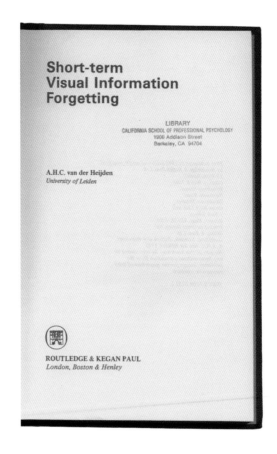

International
Library of
Psychology

Short-term Visual
Information Forgetting

A.H.C. van der Heijden

RKP

PASSING GAS: And Other Towns Along the American Highway

Gary Gladstone

Ten Speed Press, 2002

Photographic portraits of queer-sounding North-American towns and their proud inhabitants.

BITTER END
Tennessee
Terry and Jack Harrison, potato farmers

PASSING GAS
And Other Towns Along the American Highway

Portraits from the Heartland

GARY GLADSTONE

BOGS OF THE NORTHEAST

Charles W. Johnson
& Meredith Edgcomb Young

University Press of New England, 1985

Indispensable guide for connoisseurs of swamps and sloughs in Maine, New Hampshire, Vermont and beyond.

BOGS OF THE NORTHEAST

CHARLES W. JOHNSON

THE FOUL AND THE FRAGRANT: Odor and the French Social Imagination

Alain Corbin

Harvard University Press, 1986

THE

Foul

AND THE

Fragrant

ALAIN
CORBIN

Odor and the French Social Imagination

DID LEWIS CARROLL VISIT LLANDUDNO?: An Investigation

Michael Senior

Gwasg Carreg Gwalch, 2000

Rigorously argued corrective to scepticism over whether the Welsh town inspired *Alice in Wonderland.*

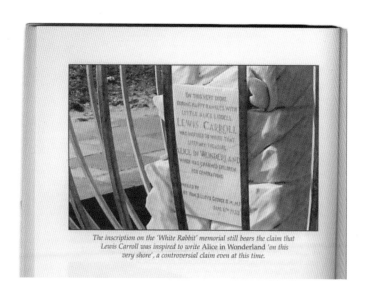

The inscription on the 'White Rabbit' memorial still bears the claim that
Lewis Carroll was inspired to write Alice in Wonderland 'on this
very shore', a controversial claim even at this time.

Did

Lewis Carroll

visit Llandudno?

Michael Senior

SHOES AND SHIT:
Stories for Pedestrians

Geoff Hancock & Rikki Ducornet (editors)

Aya Press, 1984

Highlights include 'The Shit of Knowledge',
'My Dreams are Full of Shit', and 'The Turd
as Big as a House'.

Shoes & Shit

STORIES FOR PEDESTRIANS
*An Illustrated Anthology of
Short Fiction Edited by Geoff
Hancock & Rikki Ducornet
Comprised of Selections
from the Works of Forty-five
Distinguished Writers, Poets,
Artists and Photographers
Collected & Published in
Toronto by Aya Press, 1984*

WHAT BIRD DID THAT?

The comprehensive field guide to the ornithological dejecta of Great Britain and Europe.

Peter Hansard & Burton Silver

Grub Street, 1991

Each specimen is complete with accurate calibrations of wind velocity, direction, weather conditions, time of day and measurement of spray in millimetres.

WHAT BIRD DID THAT?

The *comprehensive field guide to the ornithological dejecta of Great Britain and Europe*

Peter Hansard/Burton Silver

ALL DOGS HAVE ADHD

Kathy Hoopmann

Jessica Kingsley Publishers, 2008

Long-awaited companion to *All Cats Have Asperger's Syndrome*.

MEDITATIONS FOR CATS WHO DO TOO MUCH: Learning to Take Things One Life at a Time

Michael Cader

Penguin Books Ltd, 1993

Collection of wisdom about relaxation - for exceptional cats with reading ability.

KATHY HOOPMANN

all dogs have
ADHD

THE SECOND-HAND PARROT

Mattie Sue Athan & Dianalee Deter

Barron's Educational Series, 2002

Preparing the prospective owner for the behavioural
challenges of the adopted parrot.

Many birds will be inspired to bathe at the sound of a vacuum cleaner.

The Second-hand Parrot

A Complete Pet Owner's Manual

With a Special Chapter:
Understanding Your
Re-Homed Parrot

BARRON'S

PETROLEUM AND THE ORPHANED OSTRICH

Chris van Wyk & Gamakhulu Diniso

Ravan Press, 1988

Children's story.

PETROLEUM
and the Orphaned Ostrich
Chris van Wyk & Gamakhulu Diniso

WITHOUT REGRET: A Handbook for Owners of Canine Amputees

Susan Neal

Doral Publishing Sep 2002

WITHOUT REGRET

A Handbook for Owners of Canine Amputees

Susan Neal

GYMNASTICS: Systematic Training for Jumping Horses

James C. Wofford & Maggie Raynor

Compass Equestrian Ltd, 2002

Thankfully excludes somersaults, headstands and the splits.

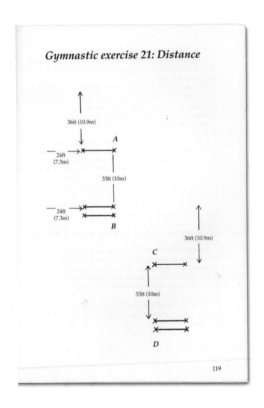

Gymnastic exercise 21: Distance

36ft (10.9m)

24ft (7.3m)

A

33ft (10m)

24ft (7.3m)

B

C

36ft (10.9m)

33ft (10m)

D

119

COMPASS
EQUESTRIAN

Points for Riders

Gymnastics

Systematic Training
for
Jumping
Horses

James C. Wofford

Concise • Compact • Comprehensive

BABOON METAPHYSICS:
The Evolution of a Social Mind

D. L. Cheney & Robert M. Seyfarth

Chicago University Press, 2008

In which you'll find Berkeley rather than Bananas in the index.

DOROTHY L. CHENEY AND ROBERT M. SEYFARTH

BABOON
METAPHYSICS

The Evolution of a Social Mind

"A captivating read." —*Nature*

ORGANIZING DEVIANCE

Joel Best & David F. Luckenbill

Prentice Hall, 1982

Analytical theory.

Organizing Deviance

Joel Best and David F. Luckenbill

ETHICS FOR BUREAUCRATS:
An Essay on Law and Values

John A. Rohr

Marcel Dekker Inc., 1989

Tackling 'the long-neglected ethical side of public decision making'.

Public Administration and Public Policy/36

ETHICS FOR BUREAUCRATS
AN ESSAY ON LAW AND VALUES

SECOND EDITION, REVISED AND EXPANDED

JOHN A. ROHR

FOREWORD BY HERBERT J. STORING

HOW TO WRITE WHILE YOU SLEEP: And Other Surprising Ways to Increase Your Writing Power

Elizabeth Irvin Ross

Writer's Digest Books, May 1987

For those looking to expand the frontier of normal writing practice.

HOW TO WRITE A HOW TO WRITE BOOK

Brian Piddock
& Anthony Connolly

Neil Rhodes Books, 2007

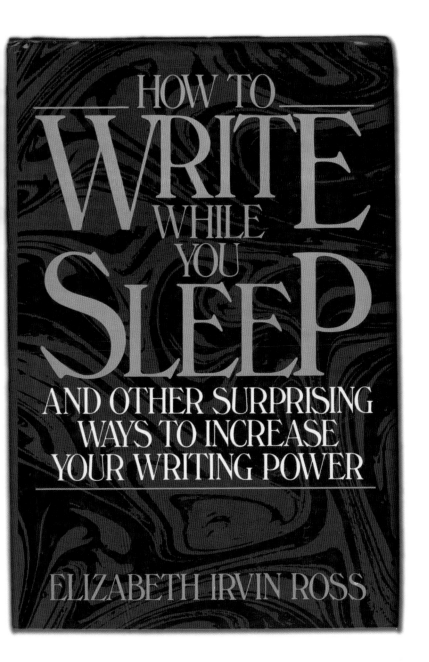

HOW TO WRITE WHILE YOU SLEEP

AND OTHER SURPRISING WAYS TO INCREASE YOUR WRITING POWER

ELIZABETH IRVIN ROSS

BEFORE AND AFTER:
The Best New Ideas for Improving the
Quality of Dying and for Inexpensive,
Green, Family-organised Funerals

Nicholas Albery

Natural Death Centre, 1995

Other helpful ideas include Coffins made of Cork and
Pots for Ashes Shaped as Beehives.

Before
And After

– The best new ideas for improving the quality of dying
and for inexpensive, green, family-organised funerals

Natural Death Centre Awards

Descriptions of Green 'd-i-y' funerals
transcending a malfunction in consciousness, tips for those
dying at home, coffins as bookcases, an Internet Garden of
Remembrance, shoulder-bag coffins

4.6

CHILDREN ARE WET CEMENT

Anne Ortlund

Fleming H Revell Co, 1995

Childrearing handbook - not to be mistaken for
Home Improvement manual.

Children are wet Cement

Anne Ortlund

IF YOU DON'T HAVE BIG BREASTS PUT RIBBONS ON YOUR PIGTAILS: And Other Lessons I Learned from My Mom

Barbara Corcoran

Portfolio, Jan 2004

IF YOU WANT CLOSURE IN YOUR RELATIONSHIP, START WITH YOUR LEGS

Big Boom

Simon Schuster, 2008

Celebrity bodyguard relinquishes pimp past, finds God and authors self-help guide for women: 'Sometimes the best communication is to be quiet.'

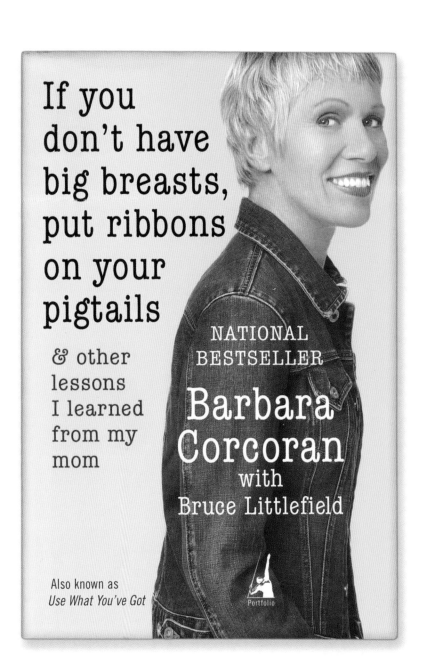

If you
don't have
big breasts,
put ribbons
on your
pigtails

& other
lessons
I learned
from my
mom

NATIONAL
BESTSELLER

**Barbara
Corcoran**

with
Bruce Littlefield

Also known as
Use What You've Got

Portfolio

ARE WOMEN HUMAN?
And Other International Dialogues

Catharine. A. MacKinnon

Harvard University Press, 2007

Collection of essays on women's rights.

are
women
human
?

And Other

International Dialogues

CATHARINE A. MacKINNON

THE SACRED AND THE FEMININE: Toward a Theology of Housework

Kathryn Allen Rabuzzi

Seabury Press, 1982

Includes chapter on 'Housework as Ritual Enactment'.

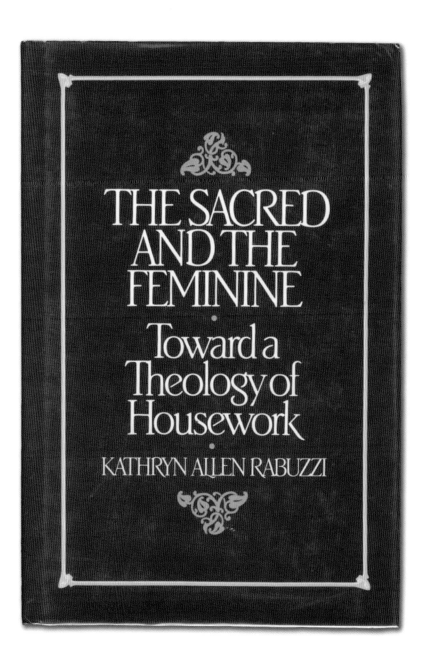

THE SACRED AND THE FEMININE

Toward a Theology of Housework

KATHRYN ALLEN RABUZZI

EVERYTHING I KNOW ABOUT WOMEN I LEARNED FROM MY TRACTOR

Roger Welsch

Motorbooks International, 2003

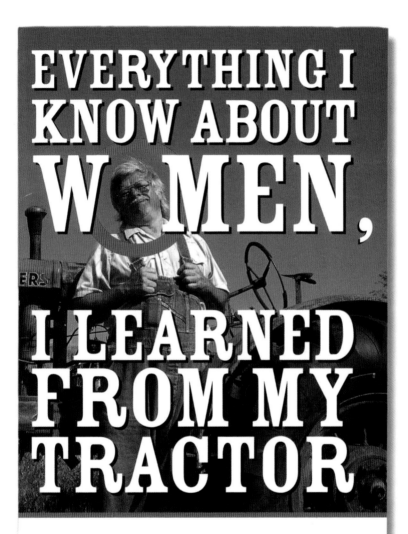

EVERYTHING I KNOW ABOUT W MEN, I LEARNED FROM MY TRACTOR

ROGER WELSCH

WHERE DO BABIES COME FROM? AND HOW TO KEEP THEM THERE!: What a Teenager Should Know About Sex, Love, Marriage, and Birth Control.

LeMon Clark

Exposition Press, 1978

Handbook for adolescents.

WHEN MEN ARE PREGNANT: Needs and Concerns of Expectant Fathers

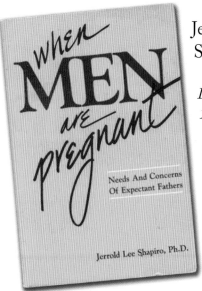

Jerrold Lee Shapiro

Impact Publishers, 1989

Handbook for expectant fathers.

Where Do Babies
Come From?
And How To
Keep Them
THERE!

RUFFLES ON MY LONGJOHNS

Isabel Edwards

Hancock House Publishers Ltd, 1994

Novel.

Ruffles on my Longjohns

by Isabel Edwards

I WAS TORTURED BY THE PYGMY LOVE QUEEN

Jasper McCutcheon

The Nazca Plains Corporation, 2007

Novel.

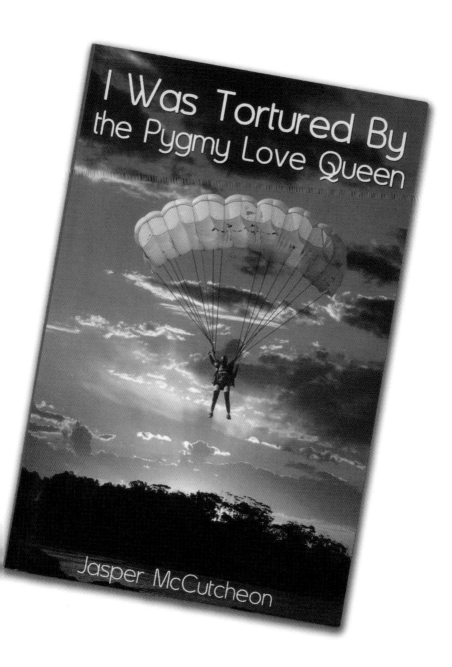

I Was Tortured By the Pygmy Love Queen

Jasper McCutcheon

KEEPING WARM WITH AN AX:
A Woodcutter's Manual

Dudley Cook

Universe Books, 1981

Complete guide for woodcutting enthusiasts.

KEEPING WARM WITH AN AX

A Woodcutter's Manual

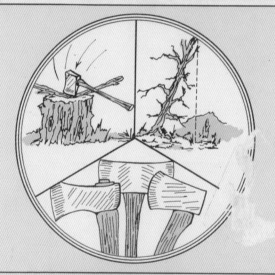

D. Cook

FLOWER DRYING WITH A MICROWAVE: Techniques and Projects

Titia Joosten

Sterling Publishing, 1989

Craft handbook.

Flower Drying
With A Microwave

Techniques and Projects

Titia Joosten

THE OFFICIAL CLUB THROWER'S HANDBOOK:
Throwing Golf Clubs for Distance and Accuracy

Tom Carey

Double Eagle Press, 1995

Includes popular techniques such as 'The Two-Iron Twist, 'The Whirlybird' and 'The Caddie-Killer'.

THE OFFICIAL
Club
Thrower's
Handbook

Tom Carey

Author of
"Teed Off! The Modern Guide To Golf!"

SEARCHING FOR RAILWAY TELEGRAPH INSULATORS

William Keith Neal

Signal Box Press, 1982

Illustrating over 140 different varieties.

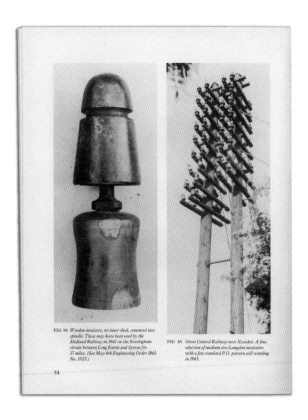

FIG 64 *Wooden insulator, no inner shed, cemented into spindle. These may have been used by the Midland Railway in 1861 on the Nottingham circuit between Long Eaton and Syston for 17 miles. (See May 4th Engineering Order 1861. No. 3523.)*

FIG 65 *Great Central Railway near Neasden. A fine selection of medium size Langdon insulators with a few standard P.O. pattern still standing in 1965.*

54

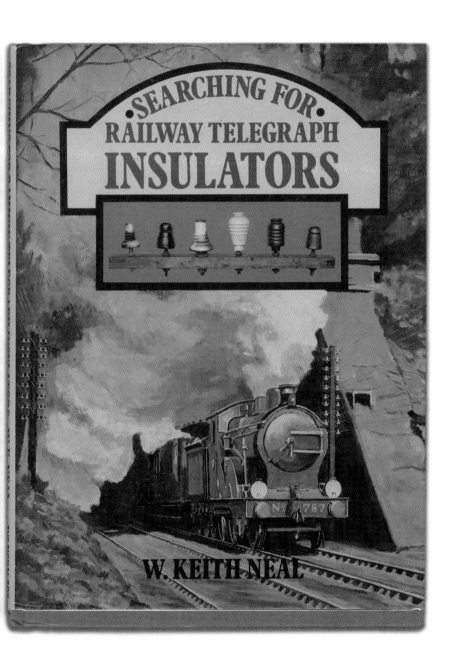

·SEARCHING FOR·
RAILWAY TELEGRAPH
INSULATORS

W. KEITH NEAL

THE HISTORY OF THE CONCRETE ROOFING TILE:
Its Origin and Development in Germany

Charles George Dobson

Batsford, 1959

Exhaustive history for concrete fans.

THE

HISTORY

OF THE

CONCRETE

ROOFING

TILE

Its Origin and Development in Germany

Charles Dobson

THE LANGUAGE OF RUBBER

Elastomer Chemicals Department

E. I. du Pont de Nemours and Company, 1963

Translating the engineering peculiarities of rubber.

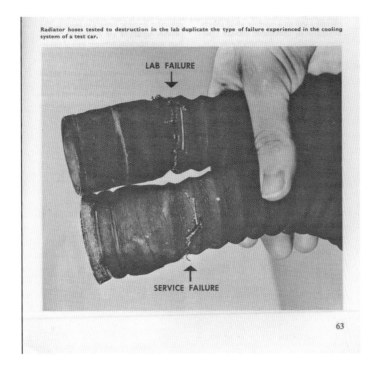

Radiator hoses tested to destruction in the lab duplicate the type of failure experienced in the cooling system of a test car.

LAB FAILURE

SERVICE FAILURE

63

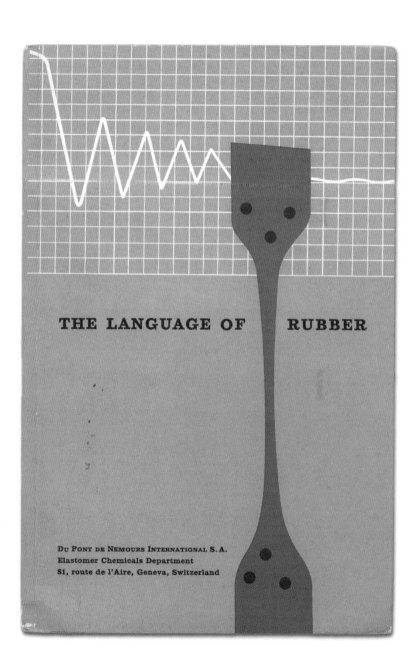

THE LANGUAGE OF   RUBBER

Du Pont de Nemours International S.A.
Elastomer Chemicals Department
81, route de l'Aire, Geneva, Switzerland

HOLDING THE LINE:
The Telephone in Old Order Mennonite and Amish Life

Prof. Diane Zimmerman Umble PhD

The Johns Hopkins University Press, 2000

Study of the impact of the telephone on the Mennonite and Amish community.

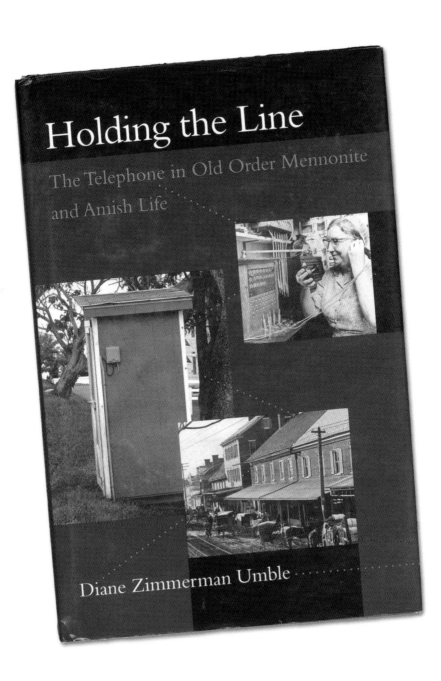

Holding the Line

The Telephone in Old Order Mennonite and Amish Life

Diane Zimmerman Umble

CANNIBALISM AND THE COMMONLAW:
A Victorian Yachting Tragedy

A. W. Brian Simpson

The Hambledon Press, 1994

Disturbing incident on British ship bound for New South Wales, which instigates new legislation.

CANNIBALISM
AND THE COMMON LAW

A Victorian Yachting Tragedy

A.W. BRIAN SIMPSON

But the winner of the 2009 Diagram Prize for Oddest Book Title of the Year is:

THE 2009-2014 OUTLOOK FOR 60-MILLIGRAM CONTAINERS OF FROMAGE FRAIS IN THE UNITED STATES

Professor Philip M. Parker, Ph.D

ICON Group International, Inc. 2009

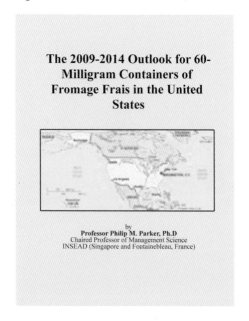

Available on Amazon for only £795 a copy.